I0409273

Table of Contents

Supply Chain 101: Understanding the Essentials of
Distribution for Business Success

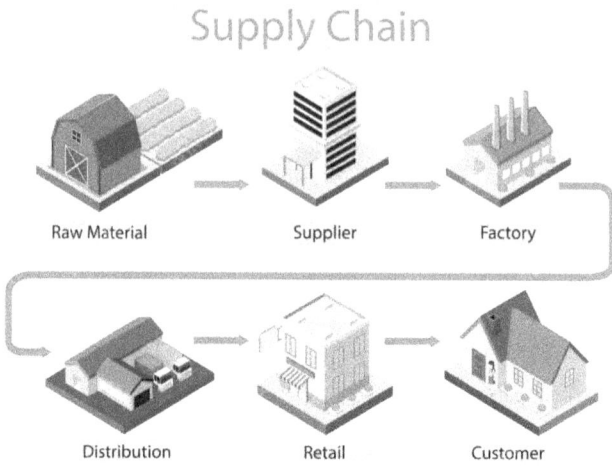

Introduction to Supply Chain Management

Supply chain management is a crucial aspect of modern
business operations, ensuring the efficient flow of goods,
services, and information from the point of origin to the point
of consumption. It encompasses a wide range of activities,
including procurement, production, transportation,
warehousing, and customer service. By effectively managing
the entire supply chain, organizations can enhance their
competitiveness, reduce costs, and improve customer
satisfaction.

The primary goal of supply chain management is to match
supply with demand. This involves forecasting customer
demand, aligning production and distribution activities
accordingly, and minimizing inventory levels while ensuring
timely delivery. By achieving this balance, organizations can

optimize their resources and respond swiftly to market changes.

An effective supply chain consists of various interconnected components, including suppliers, manufacturers, distributors, retailers, and customers. Each of these entities plays a crucial role in ensuring the smooth flow of goods and services. Collaboration and coordination among these stakeholders are essential to eliminate bottlenecks, reduce lead times, and enhance overall efficiency.

Information systems and technology play a vital role in supply chain management. They enable organizations to capture, analyze, and share data across the entire supply chain, providing real-time visibility, improving decision-making, and enhancing operational performance. Technologies such as RFID, barcode scanning, and advanced analytics have revolutionized supply chain management, enabling organizations to track inventory, monitor production processes, and optimize transportation routes.

Managing the flow of materials is another critical aspect of supply chain management. It involves efficient procurement, transportation, and warehousing of raw materials, work-in-progress inventory, and finished goods. By optimizing these processes, organizations can minimize costs, reduce lead times, and ensure the availability of products when and where they are needed.

Building and maintaining strong relationships with suppliers, manufacturers, distributors, and customers is essential for effective supply chain management. Collaborative partnerships based on trust, mutual understanding, and shared goals can lead to improved performance, increased innovation, and enhanced customer satisfaction. Regular communication, joint planning, and a focus on long-term relationships are key to developing successful supply chain relationships.

Supply chain management is not just a tactical function but also a strategic tool for achieving organizational goals. It requires a holistic approach, considering the entire value chain and aligning supply chain strategies with overall business objectives. By adopting a strategic mindset, organizations can leverage their supply chain capabilities to gain a competitive advantage, drive innovation, and create value for customers.

In conclusion, supply chain management is a complex and multifaceted discipline that plays a critical role in the success of organizations. It involves the integration of various activities, stakeholders, and technologies to ensure the efficient flow of goods, services, and information. By effectively managing the supply chain, organizations can enhance their operational performance, reduce costs, and deliver superior customer value.

The importance of supply chain management for businesses

Introduction

In today's globalized and interconnected business landscape, effective supply chain management has become increasingly crucial for businesses to thrive and remain competitive. Supply chain management entails the coordination and optimization of the flow of goods, materials, and information from suppliers to manufacturers, distributors, retailers, and ultimately, to the end consumers. This chapter explores the various reasons why supply chain management is essential for businesses and how it directly impacts their profitability and long-term success.

Cost Reduction and Operational Efficiency

One of the primary reasons why supply chain management is vital for businesses is its ability to reduce costs and improve operational efficiency. By optimizing the flow of goods, materials, and information, businesses can eliminate waste, reduce inventory carrying costs, and enhance productivity. Effective supply chain management streamlines operations minimizes idle time, and maximizes the utilization of resources, leading to significant cost savings. Moreover, it enables businesses to negotiate better terms with suppliers, resulting in lower procurement costs and better pricing agreements.

Timely and Quality Product Delivery A well-managed supply chain ensures that products are delivered to customers in a timely and efficient manner. This is achieved through effective demand planning, inventory management, and logistics coordination. By accurately forecasting demand and aligning production schedules with customer needs, businesses can avoid stockouts and minimize lead times. Timely delivery enhances customer satisfaction, fosters loyalty, and creates a positive brand image. Furthermore, supply chain management facilitates quality control processes, ensuring that products meet or exceed customer expectations, thereby enhancing customer retention and repeat purchases.

Competitive Advantage

An efficiently managed supply chain can provide businesses with a significant competitive advantage in the marketplace. By offering better prices, faster delivery times, and higher product quality, companies can differentiate themselves from competitors and attract more customers. Additionally, a well-optimized supply chain enables businesses to respond quickly to market changes and customer demands, allowing them to stay ahead of the competition. Moreover, by leveraging data analytics and technology, businesses can gain insights into customer preferences and market trends, enabling them to make informed decisions and offer tailored products and services.

Risk Mitigation and Resilience

Supply chain management plays a crucial role in identifying and mitigating potential risks and disruptions. By mapping out the entire supply chain network, businesses can identify vulnerabilities and develop contingency plans to mitigate risks such as supplier disruptions, natural disasters, or geopolitical uncertainties. Moreover, diversifying suppliers and establishing strong relationships with them can help businesses navigate unforeseen circumstances and ensure a continuous flow of goods and materials. Effective supply chain management enhances the resilience of businesses, allowing them to adapt swiftly to changing market conditions and maintain uninterrupted operations.

Collaboration and Innovation

Supply chain management fosters collaboration and innovation within and across organizations. By collaborating closely with suppliers, manufacturers, distributors, and other stakeholders, businesses can improve communication, share knowledge, and drive innovation. Collaborative efforts can lead to the development of new products, improved processes, and the adoption of sustainable and ethical practices. Furthermore, by integrating suppliers and other partners into the product development and decision-making processes, businesses can enhance the overall value proposition and create a competitive edge.

Sustainability and Ethical Practices

In today's socially conscious world, supply chain management plays a crucial role in ensuring sustainable and ethical practices. Customers are increasingly concerned about the environmental and social impact of the products they purchase. By implementing sustainable supply chain practices, such as reducing carbon emissions, minimizing waste, and promoting fair labor practices, businesses can enhance their reputation, attract environmentally and socially responsible customers, and comply with regulatory requirements.

Moreover, supply chain transparency and traceability enable businesses to ensure that their products are sourced ethically, thereby mitigating reputational risks and potential legal issues.

Conclusion

The importance of supply chain management for businesses cannot be overstated. It directly impacts profitability, operational efficiency, customer satisfaction, and long-term success. Effective supply chain management helps businesses reduce costs, ensure timely and quality product delivery, gain a competitive advantage, mitigate risks, foster collaboration and innovation, and promote sustainable and ethical practices. In today's dynamic and interconnected business environment, organizations that prioritize and invest in supply chain management are better positioned to navigate challenges, seize opportunities, and achieve sustainable growth.

Understanding the flow of goods in a supply chain.
The flow of goods in a supply chain is a critical aspect of effective supply chain management. It involves the movement of products, materials, and information from the initial stages of production to the final consumer. Understanding the flow of goods is essential for businesses to optimize their supply chain operations, improve efficiency, and enhance customer satisfaction. In this chapter, we will explore the two main types of flow in a supply chain: upstream and downstream

2.1 Upstream Flow

The upstream flow refers to the movement of goods and information from suppliers and manufacturers towards the end consumer. It encompasses the various activities involved in procuring raw materials, transforming them into finished products, and delivering them to the next stage of the supply chain. Let's take a closer look at the key components of the upstream flow:

2.1.1 Procurement

Procurement is the process of sourcing and acquiring the necessary raw materials, components, and services required for production. It involves identifying reliable suppliers, negotiating contracts, and ensuring timely delivery of materials. Effective procurement practices can significantly impact the overall efficiency and cost-effectiveness of the supply chain.

2.1.2 Production

Once the raw materials are procured, the production process begins. This stage involves transforming the raw materials into finished goods through various manufacturing processes. It includes activities such as assembly, fabrication, packaging, quality control, and inventory management. Efficient production processes are crucial for meeting customer demand, minimizing lead times, and maintaining product quality.

2.1.3 Transportation and Logistics

Transportation and logistics play a vital role in the upstream flow of goods. It involves the movement of raw materials from suppliers to manufacturers and the distribution of finished products to warehouses or retailers. Effective transportation and logistics management ensure timely delivery, minimize transportation costs, and optimize inventory levels.

2.1.4 Inventory Management

Inventory management is a critical aspect of the upstream flow. It involves maintaining optimal inventory levels to meet customer demand while minimizing carrying costs. Effective inventory management strategies include demand forecasting, safety stock management, and just-in-time (JIT) inventory systems.

2.1.5 Supplier Relationship Management

Building strong relationships with suppliers is essential for the smooth flow of goods in the upstream supply chain. Supplier relationship management focuses on fostering collaboration, communication, and trust with suppliers. It involves regular communication, performance monitoring, and continuous improvement initiatives to ensure a reliable and efficient supply of materials.

2.2 Downstream Flow

The downstream flow refers to the movement of goods and information from manufacturers towards the end consumer. It encompasses the activities involved in distributing and delivering finished products to the final destination. Let's explore the key components of the downstream flow:

2.2.1 Distribution

Distribution involves the process of allocating and delivering finished products to various channels, such as retailers, wholesalers, or directly to the end consumer. It includes activities like order processing, warehousing, transportation, and delivery. Efficient distribution processes ensure timely and accurate delivery while minimizing costs and maximizing customer satisfaction.

2.2.2 Retailing

Retailing is a crucial component of the downstream flow, especially in consumer goods supply chains. It involves the selling of products directly to the end consumer through various channels, such as brick-and-mortar stores, e-commerce platforms, or direct sales. Effective retailing strategies focus on understanding customer preferences, managing inventory, and providing exceptional customer service.

2.2.3 Customer Relationship Management

Customer relationship management (CRM) is essential in the downstream flow as it involves building and maintaining strong relationships with customers. CRM strategies aim to understand customer needs, preferences, and buying behavior to provide personalized experiences and foster loyalty. It includes activities like customer segmentation, targeted marketing, and after-sales support.

2.2.4 After-sales Service

After-sales service plays a crucial role in the downstream flow, especially for durable goods or products requiring maintenance and support. It includes activities like warranty management, technical support, repairs, and product returns. Effective after-sales service enhances customer satisfaction, builds brand loyalty, and contributes to long-term profitability.

2.3 Integration of Upstream and Downstream Flows

The successful management of the supply chain requires seamless integration of both upstream and downstream flows. The coordination and collaboration between suppliers, manufacturers, distributors, retailers, and customers are crucial for optimizing supply chain performance. Here are some key considerations for integrating upstream and downstream flows:

2.3.1 Information Sharing

Effective information sharing among supply chain partners is vital for coordinating activities and making informed decisions. Real-time visibility of inventory levels, production schedules, and customer demand enables proactive planning, reduces lead times, and minimizes the risk of stockouts or overstocking.

2.3.2 Collaboration and Partnerships

Building strong collaborative relationships with supply chain partners fosters trust, improves communication, and enhances overall supply chain performance. Collaborative initiatives like vendor-managed inventory (VMI), collaborative planning, forecasting, replenishment (CPFR), and joint product development can drive efficiency, reduce costs, and promote innovation.

2.3.3 Technology and Automation

Leveraging technology and automation tools can streamline the flow of goods in the supply chain. Advanced software systems, such as enterprise resource planning (ERP), warehouse management systems (WMS), and transportation management systems (TMS), enable real-time tracking, efficient inventory management, and automated order processing.

2.3.4 Continuous Improvement

Continuous improvement is essential in optimizing the flow of goods in the supply chain. Regular evaluation of key performance indicators (KPIs), monitoring customer feedback, and implementing process enhancements drive efficiency, reduce costs, and enhance customer satisfaction.

Conclusion

Understanding the flow of goods in a supply chain is crucial for businesses to optimize their operations, improve efficiency, and enhance customer satisfaction. The upstream flow involves procuring raw materials, production, transportation, and supplier relationship management. The downstream flow encompasses distribution, retailing, customer relationship management, and after-sales service. By integrating and optimizing both flows, businesses can achieve a competitive advantage, mitigate risks, and achieve sustainable growth in today's dynamic business environment.

Effective supply chain management is guided by several key principles that help organizations streamline their operations and achieve optimal results. These principles include:

Collaboration: Collaboration and cooperation between all stakeholders in the supply chain, including suppliers, manufacturers, distributors, and retailers, are essential for success. By sharing information, coordinating activities, and aligning goals, companies can enhance efficiency and responsiveness. This collaborative approach enables better communication, reduces lead times, minimizes inventory levels, and improves overall customer satisfaction. By working together, organizations can effectively address challenges, resolve conflicts, and achieve shared objectives.

Visibility: Having visibility and real-time information about the entire supply chain is crucial. This allows companies to identify potential bottlenecks, anticipate disruptions, and make informed decisions. With the help of advanced technologies such as RFID (Radio Frequency Identification), IoT (Internet of Things), and data analytics, organizations can track and monitor inventory, shipments, and production processes in real time. This visibility enables proactive management, reduces risks, improves inventory accuracy, and enhances overall supply chain performance.

Flexibility: The ability to adapt to changing market conditions and customer demands is a critical aspect of supply chain management. Companies that can quickly adjust their operations and processes are better prepared to handle unexpected events and maintain customer satisfaction. Flexibility in the supply chain can be achieved through strategies such as agile manufacturing, lean principles, and dynamic network optimization. By adopting these approaches, organizations can respond swiftly to market fluctuations, customize products, shorten lead times, and improve overall agility.

Continuous Improvement: Supply chain management is an ongoing process of improvement. By regularly evaluating performance, identifying areas for enhancement, and implementing changes, organizations can optimize their supply chain operations and stay ahead of the competition. Continuous improvement practices such as Lean Six Sigma, Total Quality Management (TQM), and Kaizen play a crucial role in driving efficiency and effectiveness. These methodologies enable organizations to eliminate waste, reduce costs, enhance productivity, and improve customer satisfaction. By fostering a culture of continuous improvement, organizations can create a competitive advantage and achieve sustainable growth.

Risk Management: Risk management is a fundamental principle of effective supply chain management. Companies need to identify, assess, and mitigate risks throughout the supply chain to minimize disruptions and ensure business continuity. Risk management strategies include contingency planning, dual sourcing, supply chain mapping, and developing alternative transportation routes. By proactively addressing risks such as natural disasters, supplier bankruptcies, geopolitical issues, and demand volatility, organizations can mitigate potential damages and maintain a resilient supply chain.

Sustainability: Sustainability has become a critical consideration in modern supply chain management. Organizations are increasingly focusing on environmental and social responsibility to meet customer expectations and comply with regulations. Sustainable supply chain practices include reducing carbon emissions, optimizing transportation routes, using eco-friendly packaging, promoting ethical sourcing, and supporting fair labor practices. By integrating sustainability into their supply chain strategies, organizations can enhance their brand reputation, attract environmentally conscious customers, and contribute to a greener future.

Technology Integration: Technology plays a vital role in optimizing supply chain management. Organizations are leveraging advanced technologies such as cloud computing, artificial intelligence, machine learning, and blockchain to automate processes, improve visibility, and enhance decision-making. These technologies enable real-time data analysis, predictive modeling, demand forecasting, inventory optimization, and efficient communication across the supply chain. By embracing digital transformation, organizations can achieve operational excellence, reduce costs, and gain a competitive edge in the market.

In conclusion, effective supply chain management is guided by key principles that help organizations streamline their operations and achieve optimal results. Collaboration, visibility, flexibility, continuous improvement, risk management, sustainability, and technology integration are essential for driving efficiency, responsiveness, and competitiveness in the supply chain. By embracing these principles, organizations can build resilient supply chains that can adapt to changing market dynamics, deliver superior customer experiences, and achieve long-term success.

Common challenges in supply chain management and how to overcome them.

Introduction

Supply chain management plays a critical role in the success of any organization. It involves the coordination and integration of various processes, from sourcing raw materials to delivering finished products to customers. However, managing a supply chain is not without its challenges. In this chapter, we will explore some of the common challenges faced by supply chain managers and discuss effective strategies to overcome them. By understanding and addressing these challenges, organizations can create resilient and efficient supply chains.

1. Lack of Collaboration

Collaboration is one of the key principles of effective supply chain management. However, many organizations struggle with achieving seamless collaboration between different stakeholders, including suppliers, manufacturers, distributors, and retailers. A lack of collaboration can result in delays, inefficiencies, and increased costs.

Overcoming the Challenge

To overcome this challenge, organizations can take several steps:

- **Foster a culture of collaboration:** Encourage open communication, trust, and mutual understanding among all supply chain partners.
- **Share information:** Implement robust information-sharing systems to ensure all stakeholders have access to real-time data and can make informed decisions.
- **Establish partnerships:** Build strong relationships with suppliers, manufacturers, and other partners to foster a collaborative environment.
- **Use collaboration tools:** Leverage technology solutions such as collaborative planning, forecasting, and replenishment (CPFR) systems to facilitate effective collaboration.

2. Lack of Visibility

Visibility refers to the ability to track and monitor each stage of the supply chain, from the sourcing of raw materials to the delivery of the final product. Without proper visibility, organizations may face challenges in identifying bottlenecks, anticipating disruptions, and making timely decisions.

Overcoming the Challenge

To enhance supply chain visibility, organizations can implement the following strategies:

- **Adopt advanced tracking technologies:** Utilize technologies like RFID (Radio Frequency Identification), GPS (Global Positioning System), and IoT (Internet of Things) to track and monitor inventory and shipments in real-time.
- **Implement data analytics**: Analyze supply chain data to gain insights into performance, identify areas for improvement, and predict potential disruptions.
- **Collaborate with suppliers:** Establish transparent relationships with suppliers and ensure they provide regular updates on inventory levels, lead times, and other relevant information.
- **Invest in supply chain visibility tools:** Explore supply chain visibility software and platforms that provide end-to-end visibility and can integrate with existing systems.

3. Lack of Flexibility

In today's dynamic business environment, supply chain managers must be able to adapt quickly to changing market conditions, customer demands, and unexpected events. Lack of flexibility can lead to stockouts, excess inventory, and missed opportunities.

Overcoming the Challenge

To enhance supply chain flexibility, organizations can consider the following strategies:

- **Develop agile processes:** Implement lean manufacturing principles and agile supply chain practices to enable quick response times and efficient resource allocation.
- **Establish alternative sourcing options:** Diversify the supply base and identify alternative suppliers to mitigate the risk of disruption.
- **Embrace technology:** Leverage advanced technologies such as cloud computing, automation, and robotics to optimize processes and improve flexibility.
- **Foster a culture of continuous improvement:** Encourage employees to identify and implement process improvements and embrace a mindset of continuous learning.

4. Lack of Continuous Improvement

Continuous improvement is essential for organizations to stay competitive and drive operational excellence. However, many supply chains struggle with complacency and fail to regularly evaluate and improve their processes.

Overcoming the Challenge

To foster a culture of continuous improvement in supply chain management, organizations can implement the following strategies:

- **Set performance metrics:** Define key performance indicators (KPIs) to measure and monitor supply chain performance regularly.
- **Conduct regular audits:** Perform periodic audits to identify areas for improvement and address any inefficiencies or bottlenecks.
- **Encourage employee involvement:** Involve employees at all levels in the continuous

improvement process and provide them with the necessary training and tools.

- **Embrace technology:** Leverage analytics, machine learning, and automation to identify opportunities for improvement and optimize processes.

5. Lack of Risk Management

Supply chains are vulnerable to various risks, including natural disasters, geopolitical uncertainties, supplier bankruptcies, and demand fluctuations. Failing to address these risks can result in disruptions, increased costs, and reputational damage.

Overcoming the Challenge

To effectively manage risks in the supply chain, organizations can consider the following strategies:

- **Identify and assess risks:** Conduct a comprehensive risk assessment to identify potential risks and their potential impact on the supply chain.
- **Develop contingency plans:** Create backup plans and alternative strategies to mitigate the impact of potential disruptions.
- **Build strong relationships with suppliers:** Establish relationships with multiple suppliers and maintain regular communication to better manage risks.
- **Invest in supply chain resilience:** Implement strategies such as dual sourcing, safety stocks, and redundancy to build a resilient supply chain.

6. Lack of Sustainability Practices

In today's environmentally conscious world, organizations are under increasing pressure to adopt sustainable practices in their supply chains. However, many organizations struggle with integrating sustainability into their supply chain management processes.

Overcoming the Challenge

To embrace sustainability in supply chain management, organizations can consider the following strategies:

- **Collaborate with suppliers:** Encourage suppliers to adopt sustainable practices and consider their environmental impact when selecting suppliers.
- **Optimize transportation and logistics:** Implement strategies to reduce carbon emissions, such as optimizing transportation routes, using eco-friendly packaging materials, and adopting efficient warehouse practices.
- **Implement reverse logistics:** Develop processes to handle product returns, recycling, and waste management, reducing the environmental impact of the supply chain.
- **Measure and report sustainability performance:** Establish metrics to track and report on sustainability performance, enabling continuous improvement.

7. Lack of Technology Integration

Effective supply chain management requires the integration of various technologies and systems. However, many organizations struggle with integrating disparate systems and leveraging the full potential of technology.

Overcoming the Challenge

To overcome this challenge, organizations can consider the following strategies:

- **Adopt an integrated IT infrastructure:** Implement an integrated system that connects different functions and stakeholders in the supply chain, enabling seamless information flow.

- **Leverage cloud computing:** Utilize cloud-based platforms to enable real-time data sharing, collaboration, and scalability.
- **Embrace emerging technologies:** Explore the potential of emerging technologies such as blockchain, artificial intelligence, and predictive analytics to optimize supply chain processes.
- **Provide training and support:** Ensure employees have the necessary training and support to effectively use and leverage technology in their day-to-day operations.

Conclusion

Managing a supply chain is a complex task that involves addressing numerous challenges. By recognizing and proactively addressing these challenges, organizations can build resilient and efficient supply chains that drive operational excellence and deliver superior customer value. Collaboration, visibility, flexibility, continuous improvement, risk management, sustainability, and technology integration are key principles that can help organizations overcome these challenges and achieve supply chain success. By embracing these principles and implementing effective strategies, organizations can stay ahead of the competition and thrive in today's rapidly evolving business landscape.

Technologies and tools for optimizing supply chain operations.

Introduction

In today's fast-paced and highly competitive business environment, supply chain management plays a crucial role in the success of organizations. The efficient and effective management of the entire supply chain process, from procurement to delivery, is essential for organizations to meet customer demands, reduce costs, and gain a competitive advantage. To achieve these goals, organizations are increasingly turning to technologies and tools that can optimize their supply chain operations. This chapter explores the various technologies and tools available for optimizing supply chain operations and their benefits.

The Role of Technology in Supply Chain Operations

Technology has revolutionized the way supply chains function. It has enabled organizations to streamline processes, improve visibility, enhance decision-making, and increase overall efficiency. In the context of supply chain operations, technology can be classified into three main categories: data collection and analysis, communication and collaboration, and automation and optimization.

1. Data Collection and Analysis

Data is the lifeblood of supply chain operations. Collecting and analyzing data allows organizations to gain insights into their supply chain processes, identify bottlenecks, and make data-driven decisions. Several technologies and tools facilitate data collection and analysis, including:

- **Internet of Things (IoT):** IoT devices such as sensors and RFID tags can be used to collect real-time data on inventory levels, equipment performance, and product location. This data can provide organizations with valuable insights into their supply chain operations, enabling them to optimize processes and improve efficiency.
- **Big Data Analytics:** With the increasing volume and variety of data generated by supply chain operations, organizations can leverage big data analytics tools to analyze large datasets and identify patterns, trends, and correlations. This can help in demand

forecasting, inventory management, and supplier performance evaluation.

- **Artificial Intelligence (AI) and Machine Learning (ML):** AI and ML algorithms can analyze large datasets and learn from patterns to make accurate predictions and recommendations. These technologies can be applied to optimize supply chain operations by automating demand forecasting, improving route optimization, and optimizing inventory levels.

2. Communication and Collaboration

Effective communication and collaboration are essential for successful supply chain operations. Technologies and tools that facilitate communication and collaboration among supply chain stakeholders include:

- **Supply Chain Management (SCM) Software:** SCM software provides a centralized platform for managing and coordinating supply chain activities. It enables real-time visibility into inventory levels, order status, and supplier performance, allowing for better communication and collaboration among stakeholders.
- **Collaborative Planning, Forecasting, and Replenishment (CPFR):** CPFR is a framework that enables trading partners to collaborate on demand forecasting, inventory planning, and order replenishment. CPFR software facilitates real-time data sharing and collaboration, leading to improved forecast accuracy and reduced inventory costs.
- **Customer Relationship Management (CRM) Systems:** CRM systems help organizations manage customer relationships and improve customer service. By integrating CRM systems with supply chain operations, organizations can gain insights into customer demand patterns, preferences, and

feedback, enabling them to tailor their supply chain processes accordingly.

3. Automation and Optimization

Automation and optimization technologies can significantly improve the efficiency and effectiveness of supply chain operations. Some key technologies and tools in this category include:

- **Warehouse Management Systems (WMS):** WMS automates and optimizes warehouse operations, including receiving, put-away, picking, packing, and shipping. It improves inventory accuracy, reduces order cycle time, and enhances warehouse productivity.
- **Transportation Management Systems (TMS):** TMS optimizes transportation operations by automating route planning, carrier selection, and load optimization. It helps organizations reduce transportation costs, improve delivery accuracy, and enhance customer satisfaction.
- **Robotic Process Automation (RPA):** RPA software can automate repetitive and rule-based tasks in supply chain operations, such as order processing, invoice matching, and data entry. It reduces errors, improves process efficiency, and frees up resources for more value-added activities.

Benefits of Technology Adoption in Supply Chain Operations

The adoption of technologies and tools for optimizing supply chain operations brings several benefits to organizations. Some of the key benefits include:

- **Improved Efficiency:** Technology streamlines supply chain processes, reduces manual errors, and automates repetitive tasks, leading to improved efficiency and productivity.

- **Enhanced Visibility:** Technologies such as IoT, big data analytics, and SCM software provide real-time visibility into supply chain operations, enabling organizations to track inventory levels, monitor production processes, and identify bottlenecks.
- **Better Decision-Making:** Data-driven insights generated by technology enable organizations to make informed decisions and optimize supply chain processes. This leads to improved demand forecasting, inventory management, and supplier selection.
- **Cost Reduction:** Technology adoption can help organizations reduce costs in various ways, such as optimizing transportation routes, minimizing inventory carrying costs, and improving order accuracy.
- **Improved Customer Service:** By optimizing supply chain operations, organizations can ensure timely and accurate delivery of products, leading to improved customer satisfaction and loyalty.
- **Risk Mitigation:** Technologies such as predictive analytics and AI can help organizations identify and mitigate supply chain risks, such as disruptions in supply, demand fluctuations, and quality issues.

Challenges in Technology Adoption

While technology adoption offers numerous benefits to supply chain operations, organizations also face several challenges in implementing and integrating these technologies. Some common challenges include:

- **Cost:** Implementing technology solutions can be expensive, especially for small and medium-sized enterprises (SMEs). Organizations need to carefully evaluate the return on investment (ROI) and consider the long-term benefits before making significant investments.

- **Data Integration:** Supply chain operations generate vast amounts of data from various sources. Integrating and harmonizing this data from different systems can be a complex and time-consuming process.
- **Legacy Systems**: Many organizations still rely on legacy systems that may not be compatible with new technologies. Migrating from legacy systems to modern technologies can be challenging and require careful planning.
- **Change Management:** Implementing new technologies often requires changes in existing processes, workflows, and organizational culture. Resistance to change from employees and stakeholders can hinder the successful adoption of technology solutions.
- **Data Security and Privacy:** With the increasing reliance on technology, organizations need to ensure the security and privacy of their supply chain data. Cybersecurity threats and data breaches can have severe implications for supply chain operations.

Strategies for Successful Technology Adoption

To overcome these challenges and successfully adopt technologies for optimizing supply chain operations, organizations can follow certain strategies:

- **Assess and Prioritize:** Organizations should conduct a thorough assessment of their supply chain operations, identify pain points, and prioritize areas that can benefit the most from technology adoption. This helps in focusing resources and efforts on areas that offer maximum impact.
- **Collaboration and Change Management:** Involving key stakeholders, including employees,

suppliers, and customers, in the technology adoption process is crucial. Clear communication, training, and change management initiatives can help overcome resistance and ensure successful implementation.

- **Start Small and Scale Up:** Organizations can begin by implementing technology solutions on a smaller scale, focusing on specific processes or departments. This allows for testing, gathering feedback, and fine-tuning before scaling up the technology adoption across the entire supply chain.
- **Partnerships and Collaboration:** Collaborating with technology providers, consultants, and industry experts can help organizations navigate the complexities of technology adoption. Partnerships can provide access to expertise, resources, and best practices.
- **Data Governance and Security:** Organizations need to establish robust data governance policies and ensure data security and privacy. This includes implementing cybersecurity measures, data backup and recovery plans, and complying with relevant regulations.
- **Continuous Improvement:** Technology adoption is an ongoing process. Organizations should continuously monitor and evaluate the performance of technology solutions, gather feedback, and make necessary improvements to optimize supply chain operations further.

Conclusion

Technology has become an integral part of optimizing supply chain operations. From data collection and analysis to communication and collaboration and automation and optimization, various technologies and tools offer significant benefits to organizations. However, challenges such as cost, data integration, legacy systems, change management, and data security need to be addressed for successful technology adoption. By following strategies such as assessment and prioritization, collaboration and change management, starting small and scaling up, partnerships and collaboration, data governance and security, and continuous improvement, organizations can harness the power of technology to optimize their supply chain operations, drive efficiency, and deliver superior customer value.

Best practices in supply chain management

Supply chain management is a critical aspect of any business operation, encompassing the planning, sourcing, manufacturing, and delivery of products or services to the end customer. In today's globalized and interconnected world, organizations face numerous challenges in managing their supply chains effectively. However, by adopting best practices, businesses can optimize their supply chain operations and gain a competitive advantage. This chapter explores some of the key best practices in supply chain management and provides insights into their implementation and benefits.

1. Collaboration

Collaboration is a fundamental principle in supply chain management. It involves establishing strong relationships and partnerships with suppliers, customers, and other stakeholders to improve coordination and information sharing. By collaborating effectively, organizations can enhance communication, reduce lead times, and improve overall supply chain efficiency. Some best practices for collaboration include:

- Establishing clear communication channels and protocols.

- Sharing demand forecasts and production plans with suppliers.
- Implementing collaborative planning, forecasting, and replenishment (CPFR) strategies.
- Developing long-term relationships with key suppliers to foster trust and commitment.
- Engaging in regular performance reviews and feedback sessions with partners.

2. Visibility

Supply chain visibility refers to the ability to track and monitor inventory, orders, and shipments across the entire supply chain network. It provides real-time insights into the status of each process, enabling proactive decision-making and risk mitigation. Enhanced visibility can help organizations identify bottlenecks, minimize disruptions, and optimize inventory levels. Here are some best practices for achieving supply chain visibility:

Utilizing advanced technologies such as Internet of Things (IoT) sensors, RFID tags, and barcode scanning to track goods.

- Implementing supply chain visibility software solutions to monitor and analyze data.
- Sharing real-time information with partners through cloud-based platforms.
- Utilizing data analytics and reporting tools to gain actionable insights.
- Implementing Key Performance Indicators (KPIs) to measure and monitor supply chain performance.

3. Flexibility

In today's dynamic business environment, supply chains need to be adaptable and flexible to respond quickly to changing market conditions. Flexibility allows organizations to meet customer demands, handle disruptions, and seize new opportunities. Here are some best practices for enhancing supply chain flexibility:

- Implementing agile manufacturing processes that enable quick product changes.
- Developing a flexible network of suppliers and contract manufacturers.
- Maintaining buffer inventory to handle demand fluctuations.
- Implementing cross-training programs to ensure flexibility in the workforce.
- Investing in flexible transportation and distribution strategies.

4. Continuous Improvement

Continuous improvement is a core principle of supply chain management. It involves constantly evaluating and enhancing processes to enhance efficiency, reduce waste, and increase customer satisfaction. By adopting a culture of continuous improvement, organizations can stay ahead of the competition and achieve operational excellence. Some best practices for continuous improvement include:

- Implementing Lean Six Sigma methodologies to identify and eliminate waste.
- Conducting regular performance audits and process reviews.
- Encouraging employee involvement and empowerment in process improvement initiatives.
- Implementing a system for collecting and analyzing customer feedback.
- Benchmarking against industry leaders and adopting best practices.

5. Risk Management

Supply chains are susceptible to various risks, including natural disasters, geopolitical instability, supplier failures, and demand fluctuations. Effective risk management practices help organizations identify, assess, and mitigate these risks to ensure continuity and resilience. Here are some best practices for managing supply chain risks:

- Conducting risk assessments and creating a contingency plan.
- Diversifying the supplier base to reduce dependency on a single source.
- Developing a business continuity plan to handle disruptions.
- Monitoring and analyzing geopolitical and economic trends that may impact the supply chain.
- Collaborating with suppliers to ensure risk management practices are implemented across the entire supply chain.

6. Sustainability

Sustainability has become a key focus area for supply chain management in recent years. Organizations are increasingly expected to adopt environmentally responsible practices and contribute to social and economic well-being. By integrating sustainability into their supply chains, organizations can reduce their environmental footprint, enhance brand reputation, and attract environmentally conscious customers. Here are some best practices for sustainable supply chain management:

- Conducting a life cycle analysis of products to identify opportunities for improvement.
- Reducing waste and promoting recycling and reuse.
- Opting for greener transportation methods, such as rail or sea freight.

- Collaborating with suppliers to ensure compliance with ethical and environmental standards.
- Engaging in corporate social responsibility initiatives and community development projects.

7. Technology Integration

Technology plays a crucial role in optimizing supply chain operations. Advanced technologies enable automation, data analysis, and real-time monitoring, leading to improved efficiency and decision-making. Here are some best practices for integrating technology into supply chain management:

- Adopting a robust Enterprise Resource Planning (ERP) system to integrate various functions and processes.
- Implementing cloud-based platforms for seamless collaboration and data sharing.
- Utilizing predictive analytics and Artificial Intelligence (AI) for demand forecasting and inventory optimization.
- Embracing automation technologies such as robotics and autonomous vehicles for improved efficiency.
- Ensuring data governance and security to protect sensitive supply chain information.

Conclusion

Implementing best practices in supply chain management is essential for organizations to achieve operational excellence and gain a competitive advantage. Collaboration, visibility, flexibility, continuous improvement, risk management, sustainability, and technology integration are key principles that can drive supply chain success. By embracing these practices, businesses can enhance efficiency, reduce costs, improve customer satisfaction, and mitigate risks. However, it is important to remember that each organization's supply chain is unique, and the adoption of these best practices should be tailored to specific requirements and goals.

Conclusion: The future of supply chain management

In this book, we have explored the vast landscape of supply chain management, delving into its principles, challenges, and best practices. We have witnessed the evolution of supply chain management from a mere logistical function to a critical strategic discipline that drives operational excellence and competitive advantage. As we conclude our journey, it is important to reflect on the future of supply chain management and the transformative impact it will have on businesses and industries worldwide.

One of the key drivers shaping the future of supply chain management is technology integration. The rapid advancement of technology is revolutionizing the way supply chains operate, opening up new possibilities and opportunities for organizations. By embracing technological innovations, companies can streamline their operations, enhance efficiency, and deliver superior customer experiences.

One crucial aspect of optimizing supply chain operations is the adoption of an Enterprise Resource Planning (ERP) system. ERP systems enable organizations to integrate and automate various business processes, from procurement to inventory management, production planning to order fulfillment. By centralizing data and providing real-time visibility across the supply chain, ERP systems empower companies to make informed decisions, improve collaboration, and enhance overall performance.

Another significant advancement in technology that will shape the future of supply chain management is the implementation of cloud-based platforms. Cloud computing offers unparalleled scalability, flexibility, and accessibility, allowing organizations to seamlessly connect and collaborate with suppliers, partners, and customers across geographical boundaries. Cloud-based platforms provide real-time data analytics, supply chain visibility, and collaboration tools, enabling organizations to respond swiftly to market changes, optimize inventory levels, and enhance customer service.

Predictive analytics and artificial intelligence (AI) will also play a crucial role in the future of supply chain management. By leveraging historical and real-time data, organizations can employ predictive analytics to forecast demand, optimize inventory levels, and improve production planning. AI technologies, such as machine learning algorithms and intelligent automation, can automate routine tasks, optimize routing and scheduling, and enhance decision-making processes. These advancements will empower organizations to make data-driven decisions, increase agility, and proactively respond to customer needs.

Furthermore, the future of supply chain management will see a significant shift towards embracing automation technologies. Robotics, autonomous vehicles, and drones are already making their mark in supply chain operations, revolutionizing warehousing, transportation, and last-mile delivery. Automation technologies not only enhance operational efficiency but also improve safety, reduce costs, and minimize errors. By automating repetitive and manual tasks, organizations can free up their workforce to focus on value-added activities and strategic initiatives.

While technology integration offers numerous benefits, it is crucial to ensure data governance and security in supply chain operations. With the increasing interconnectedness and digitization of supply chains, organizations must prioritize data privacy, protection, and compliance. Implementing robust data governance practices, cybersecurity measures, and encryption protocols will safeguard sensitive information, mitigate risks, and build trust among stakeholders.

In conclusion, the future of supply chain management holds immense potential for organizations willing to embrace change and leverage technological advancements. By adopting best practices such as integrating ERP systems, implementing cloud-based platforms, utilizing predictive analytics and AI, embracing automation technologies, and ensuring data governance and security, companies can achieve operational excellence and gain a competitive advantage.

As we look ahead, it is evident that supply chain management will continue to evolve, driven by technological innovations, changing customer expectations, and global market dynamics. Organizations must remain agile, adaptable, and forward-thinking to navigate the complexities and uncertainties of the future. By staying abreast of emerging trends, embracing innovation, and continuously improving their supply chain practices, businesses can position themselves at the forefront of the industry and thrive in the ever-evolving landscape of supply chain management.